THE CONSTITUTION

OF

THE EMPIRE OF JAPAN, 1889

BY

JAPAN Country

CONSTITUTION OF THE EMPIRE OF JAPAN, 1889

Imperial Oath Sworn in the Sanctuary in the Imperial Palace
(Tsuge-bumi)

We, the Successor to the prosperous Throne of Our Predecessors, do humbly and solemnly swear to the Imperial Founder of Our House and to Our other Imperial Ancestors that, in pursuance of a great policy co-extensive with the Heavens and with the Earth, We shall maintain and secure from decline the ancient form of government.

In consideration of the progressive tendency of the course of human affairs and in parallel with the advance of civilization, We deem it expedient, in order to give clearness and distinctness to the instructions bequeathed by the Imperial Founder of Our House and by Our other Imperial Ancestors, to establish fundamental laws formulated into express provisions of law, so that, on the one hand, Our Imperial posterity may possess an express guide for the course they are to follow, and that, on the other, Our subjects shall thereby be enabled to enjoy a wider range of action in giving Us their support, and that the observance of Our laws shall continue to the remotest ages of time. We will thereby to give greater firmness to the stability of Our country and to promote the welfare of all the people within the boundaries of Our dominions; and We now establish the Imperial House Law and the Constitution. These Laws come to only an exposition of grand precepts for the conduct of the government, bequeathed by the Imperial Founder of Our House and by Our other Imperial Ancestors. That we have been so fortunate in Our reign, in keeping with the tendency of the times, as to accomplish this work, We owe to the glorious Spirits of the Imperial Founder of Our House and of Our other Imperial Ancestors.

We now reverently make Our prayer to Them and to Our Illustrious Father, and implore the help of Their Sacred Spirits, and make to Them solemn oath never at this time nor in the future to fail to be an example to our subjects in the observance of the Laws hereby established.

May the heavenly Spirits witness this Our solemn Oath.

Imperial Rescript on the Promulgation of the Constitution

Whereas We make it the joy and glory of Our heart to behold the prosperity of Our country, and the welfare of Our subjects, We do hereby, in virtue of the Supreme power We inherit from Our Imperial Ancestors, promulgate the present immutable fundamental law, for the sake of Our present subjects and their descendants.

The Imperial Founder of Our House and Our other Imperial ancestors, by the help and support of the forefathers of Our subjects, laid the foundation of Our Empire upon a basis, which is to last forever. That this brilliant achievement embellishes the annals of Our country, is due to the glorious virtues of Our Sacred Imperial ancestors, and to the loyalty and bravery of Our subjects, their love of their country and their public spirit. Considering that Our subjects are the descendants of the loyal and good subjects of Our Imperial Ancestors, We doubt not but that Our subjects will be guided by Our views, and will sympathize with all Our endeavors, and that, harmoniously cooperating together, they will share with Us Our hope of making manifest the glory of Our country, both at home and abroad, and of securing forever the stability of the work bequeathed to Us by Our Imperial Ancestors.

Preamble [or Edict] (Joyu)

Having, by virtue of the glories of Our Ancestors, ascended the throne of a lineal succession unbroken for ages eternal; desiring to promote the welfare of, and to give development to the moral and intellectual faculties of Our beloved subjects, the very same that have been favored with the benevolent care and affectionate vigilance of Our Ancestors; and hoping to maintain the prosperity of the State, in concert with Our people and with their support, We hereby promulgate, in pursuance of Our Imperial Rescript of the 12th day of the 10th month of the 14th year of Meiji, a fundamental law of the State, to exhibit the principles, by which We are guided in Our conduct, and to point out to what Our descendants and Our subjects and their descendants are forever to conform.

The right of sovereignty of the State, We have inherited from Our Ancestors, and We shall bequeath them to Our descendants. Neither We nor they shall in the future fail to wield them, in accordance with the provisions of the Constitution hereby granted.

We now declare to respect and protect the security of the rights and of the property of Our people, and to secure to them the complete enjoyment of the same, within the extent of the provisions of the present Constitution and of the law.

The Imperial Diet shall first be convoked for the 23rd year of Meiji and the time of its opening shall be the date, when the present Constitution comes into force.

When in the future it may become necessary to amend any of the provisions of the present Constitution, We or Our successors shall assume the initiative right, and submit a project for the same to the Imperial Diet. The Imperial Diet shall pass its vote upon it, according to the conditions imposed by the present Constitution, and in no otherwise shall Our descendants or Our subjects be permitted to attempt any alteration thereof.

Our Ministers of State, on Our behalf, shall be held responsible for the carrying out of the present Constitution, and Our present and future subjects shall forever assume the duty of allegiance to the present Constitution.

CHAPTER I. THE EMPEROR

Article 1. The Empire of Japan shall be reigned over and governed by a line of Emperors unbroken for ages eternal.

Article 2. The Imperial Throne shall be succeeded to by Imperial male descendants, according to the provisions of the Imperial House Law.

Article 3. The Emperor is sacred and inviolable.

Article 4. The Emperor is the head of the Empire, combining in Himself the rights of sovereignty, and exercises them, according to the provisions of the present Constitution.

Article 5. The Emperor exercises the legislative power with the consent of the Imperial Diet.

Article 6. The Emperor gives sanction to laws, and orders them to be promulgated and executed.

Article 7. The Emperor convokes the Imperial Diet, opens, closes, and prorogues it, and dissolves the House of Representatives.

Article 8. The Emperor, in consequence of an urgent necessity to maintain public safety or to avert public calamities, issues, when the Imperial Diet is not sitting, Imperial ordinances in the place of law.

(2) Such Imperial Ordinances are to be laid before the Imperial Diet at its next session, and when the Diet does not approve the said Ordinances, the Government shall declare them to be invalid for the future.

Article 9. The Emperor issues or causes to be issued, the Ordinances necessary for the carrying out of the laws, or for the maintenance of the public peace and order, and for the promotion of the welfare of the subjects. But no Ordinance shall in any way alter any of the existing laws.

Article 10. The Emperor determines the organization of the different branches of the administration, and salaries of all civil and military officers, and appoints and dismisses the same. Exceptions especially provided for in the present Constitution or in other laws, shall be in accordance with the respective provisions (bearing thereon).

Article 11. The Emperor has the supreme command of the Army and Navy.

Article 12. The Emperor determines the organization and peace standing of the Army and Navy.

Article 13. The Emperor declares war, makes peace, and concludes treaties.

Article 14. The Emperor declares a state of siege.

(2) The conditions and effects of a state of siege shall be determined by law.

Article 15. The Emperor confers titles of nobility, rank, orders and other marks of honor.

Article 16. The Emperor orders amnesty, pardon, commutation of punishments and rehabilitation.

Article 17. A Regency shall be instituted in conformity with the provisions of the Imperial House Law.

(2) The Regent shall exercise the powers appertaining to the Emperor in His name.

CHAPTER II. RIGHTS AND DUTIES OF SUBJECTS

Article 18. The conditions necessary for being a Japanese subject shall be determined by law.

Article 19. Japanese subjects may, according to qualifications determined in laws or ordinances, be appointed to civil or military or any other public offices equally.

Article 20. Japanese subjects are amenable to service in the Army or Navy, according to the provisions of law.

Article 21. Japanese subjects are amenable to the duty of paying taxes, according to the provisions of law.

Article 22. Japanese subjects shall have the liberty of abode and of changing the same within the limits of the law.

Article 23. No Japanese subject shall be arrested, detained,
tried or punished, unless according to law.

Article 24. No Japanese subject shall be deprived of his
right of being tried by the judges determined by law.

Article 25. Except in the cases provided for in the law, the house of no Japanese subject shall be entered or searched without his consent.

Article 26. Except in the cases mentioned in the law, the secrecy of the letters of every Japanese subject shall remain inviolate.

Article 27. The right of property of every Japanese subject
shall remain inviolate.

(2) Measures necessary to be taken for the public benefit
shall be any provided for by law.

Article 28. Japanese subjects shall, within limits not prejudicial to peace and order, and not antagonistic to their duties as subjects, enjoy freedom of religious belief.

Article 29. Japanese subjects shall, within the limits of law, enjoy the liberty of speech, writing, publication, public meetings and associations.

Article 30. Japanese subjects may present petitions, by observing the proper forms of respect, and by complying with the rules specially provided for the same.

Article 31. The provisions contained in the present Chapter shall not affect the exercises of the powers appertaining to the Emperor, in times of war or in cases of a national emergency.

Article 32. Each and every one of the provisions contained in the preceding Articles of the present Chapter, that are not in conflict with the laws or the rules and discipline of the Army and Navy, shall apply to the officers and men of the Army and of the Navy.

CHAPTER III. THE IMPERIAL DIET

Article 33. The Imperial Diet shall consist of two Houses, a House of Peers and a House of Representatives.

Article 34. The House of Peers shall, in accordance with the ordinance concerning the House of Peers, be composed of the members of the Imperial Family, of the orders of nobility, and of those who have been nominated thereto by the Emperor.

Article 35. The House of Representatives shall be composed of members elected by the people, according to the provisions of the law of Election.

Article 36. No one can at one and the same time be a Member of both Houses.

Article 37. Every law requires the consent of the Imperial Diet.

Article 38. Both Houses shall vote upon projects of law submitted to it by the Government, and may respectively initiate projects of law.

Article 39. A Bill, which has been rejected by either the one or the other of the two Houses, shall not be brought in again during the same session.

Article 40. Both Houses can make representations to the Government, as to laws or upon any other subject. When, however, such representations are not accepted, they cannot be made a second time during the same session.

Article 41. The Imperial Diet shall be convoked every year.

Article 42. A session of the Imperial Diet shall last during three months. In case of necessity, the duration of a session may be prolonged by the Imperial Order.

Article 43. When urgent necessity arises, an extraordinary
session may be convoked in addition to the ordinary one.

(2) The duration of an extraordinary session shall be
determined by Imperial Order.

Article 44. The opening, closing, prolongation of session and prorogation of the Imperial Diet, shall be effected simultaneously for both Houses.

(2) In case the House of Representatives has been ordered to dissolve, the House of Peers shall at the same time be prorogued.

Article 45. When the House of Representatives has been ordered to dissolve, Members shall be caused by Imperial Order to be newly elected, and the new House shall be convoked within five months from the day of dissolution.

Article 46. No debate can be opened and no vote can be taken in either House of the Imperial Diet, unless not less than one-third of the whole number of Members thereof is present.

Article 47. Votes shall be taken in both Houses by absolute majority. In the case of a tie vote, the President shall have the casting vote.

Article 48. The deliberations of both Houses shall be held in public. The deliberations may, however, upon demand of the Government or by resolution of the House, be held in secret sitting.

Article 49. Both Houses of the Imperial Diet may respectively present addresses to the Emperor.

Article 50. Both Houses may receive petitions presented   by subjects.

Article 51. Both Houses may enact, besides what is provided for in the present Constitution and in the Law of the Houses, rules necessary for the management of their internal affairs.

Article 52. No Member of either House shall be held responsible outside the respective Houses, for any opinion uttered or for any vote given in the House. When, however, a Member himself has given publicity to his opinions by public speech, by documents in print or in writing, or by any other similar means, he shall, in the matter, be amenable to the general law.

Article 53. The Members of both Houses shall, during the session, be free from arrest, unless with the consent of the House, except in cases of flagrant delicts, or of offenses connected with a state of internal commotion or with a foreign trouble.

Article 54. The Ministers of State and the Delegates of the Government may, at any time, take seats and speak in either House.

CHAPTER IV. THE MINISTERS OF STATE AND THE PRIVY COUNCIL

Article 55. The respective Ministers of State shall give their advice to the Emperor, and be responsible for it.

(2) All Laws, Imperial Ordinances, and Imperial Rescripts of whatever kind, that relate to the affairs of the state, require the countersignature of a Minister of State.

Article 56. The Privy Councillors shall, in accordance with the provisions for the organization of the Privy Council, deliberate upon important matters of State when they have been consulted by the Emperor.

CHAPTER V. THE JUDICATURE

Article 57. The Judicature shall be exercised by the   Courts of Law according to law, in the name of the Emperor.

(2) The organization of the Courts of Law shall be determined by law.

Article 58. The judges shall be appointed from among   those, who possess proper qualifications according to law.

(2) No judge shall be deprived of his position, unless   by way of criminal sentence or disciplinary punishment.

(3) Rules for disciplinary punishment shall be determined   by law.

Article 59. Trials and judgments of a Court shall be conducted publicly. When, however, there exists any fear, that such publicity may be prejudicial to peace and order, or to the maintenance of public morality, the public trial may be suspended by provisions of law or by the decision of the Court of Law.

Article 60. All matters that fall within the competency of a special Court, shall be specially provided for by law.

Article 61. No suit at law, which relates to rights alleged to have been infringed by the illegal measures of the administrative authorities, and which shall come within the competency of the Court of Administrative Litigation specially established by law, shall be taken cognizance of by Court of Law.

CHAPTER VI. FINANCE

Article 62. The imposition of a new tax or the modification of the rates (of an existing one) shall be determined by law.

(2) However, all such administrative fees or other revenue having the nature of compensation shall not fall within the category of the above clause.

(3) The raising of national loans and the contracting of other liabilities to the charge of the National Treasury, except those that are provided in the Budget, shall require the consent of the Imperial Diet.

Article 63. The taxes levied at present shall, in so far as they are not remodelled by a new law, be collected according to the old system.

Article 64. The expenditure and revenue of the State require the consent of the Imperial Diet by means of an annual Budget.

(2) Any and all expenditures overpassing the appropriations set forth in the Titles and Paragraphs of the Budget, or that are not provided for in the Budget, shall subsequently require the approbation of the Imperial Diet.

Article 65. The Budget shall be first laid before the House of Representatives.

Article 66. The expenditures of the Imperial House shall be defrayed every year out of the National Treasury, according to the present fixed amount for the same, and shall not require the consent thereto of the Imperial Diet, except in case an increase thereof is found necessary.

Article 67. Those already fixed expenditures based by the Constitution upon the powers appertaining to the Emperor, and such expenditures as may have arisen by the effect of law, or that appertain to the legal obligations of the Government, shall be neither rejected nor reduced by the Imperial Diet, without the concurrence of the Government.

Article 68. In order to meet special requirements, the Government may ask the consent of the Imperial Diet to a certain amount as a Continuing Expenditure Fund, for a previously fixed number of years.

Article 69. In order to supply deficiencies, which are unavoidable, in the Budget, and to meet requirements unprovided for in the same, a Reserve Fund shall be provided in the Budget.

Article 70. When the Imperial Diet cannot be convoked, owing to the external or internal condition of the country, in case of urgent need for the maintenance of public safety, the Government may take all necessary financial measures, by means of an Imperial Ordinance.

(2) In the case mentioned in the preceding clause, the matter shall be submitted to the Imperial Diet at its next session, and its approbation shall be obtained thereto.

Article 71. When the Imperial Diet has not voted on the Budget, or when the Budget has not been brought into actual existence, the Government shall carry out the Budget of the preceding year.

Article 72. The final account of the expenditures and revenues of the State shall be verified and confirmed by the Board of Audit, and it shall be submitted by the Government to the Imperial Diet, together with the report of verification of the said board.

(2) The organization and competency of the Board of Audit shall of determined by law separately.

CHAPTER VII. SUPPLEMENTARY RULES

Article 73. When it has become necessary in future to amend the provisions of the present Constitution, a project to the effect shall be submitted to the Imperial Diet by Imperial Order.

(2) In the above case, neither House can open the debate, unless not less than two-thirds of the whole number of Members are present, and no amendment can be passed, unless a majority of not less than two-thirds of the Members present is obtained.

Article 74. No modification of the Imperial House Law shall be required to be submitted to the deliberation of the Imperial Diet.

(2) No provision of the present Constitution can be modified by the Imperial House Law.

Article 75. No modification can be introduced into the Constitution, or into the Imperial House Law, during the time of a Regency.

Article 76. Existing legal enactments, such as laws, regulations, Ordinances, or by whatever names they may be called, shall, so far as they do not conflict with the present Constitution, continue in force.

(2) All existing contracts or orders, that entail obligations upon the Government, and that are connected with expenditure, shall come within the scope of Article 67.

(The above is the semi-official translation, which appeared in H. Ito, Commentaries on the Constitution of the Empire of Japan, trans. M. Ito, 1889.)

End of the book.